Through These Lenses

Through These Lenses

by
Apostolos Anagnostopoulos

and with illustrations by
Eric Theodoropoulos

Probato
Publishing

SECOND PRINTING, DECEMBER 2013

Copyright © 2010 by Apostolos Anagnostopoulos

Through These Lenses

All rights reserved. No part of this publication may be reproduced, stored in a retrieval system, or transmitted in any form or by any means, electronic, mechanical, photocopying, recording, or otherwise, without prior permission of the publisher. All characters appearing in this work are fictitious. Any resemblance to real persons, living or dead, is purely coincidental. Published in the United States by Probato Publishing, New York.

Typeset in Perpetua.

ISBN-13: 978-0615782256
ISBN-10: 0615782256
Printed in the United States of America

10 9 8 7 6 5 4 3 2 1

DEDICATION

To my sister, Stacy. May everything you wish for come true.

To the members of Neopoet that helped make me a better person.

To Paul, Andrew, Eric, Rett, Katie and Nina and all those who worked diligently to make this publication a reality.

CONTENTS

Birth of a Dream 1

Chapter 1: Through These Lenses 3

Through These Lenses 4
To the Poet 5
Standing Ovation 6
Dear Mr. President 7
Political Prostitution 8
A Simple Song 10
Weary Traveler 11
A Day in New York 12
No Surprise 13
American Dream 14
A Moment 15
Actress 16
Adrenaline 17
At Peace 18
Monster 19
Russian Roulette 20
Your Performance 21
Predators 22
Collateral Damage 23
Classified section 24
Forgotten Boulevards 25
Unspoken 26

Chapter 2: Windows of a Soul 29

The Few Good Hearted 30
Lady Love 31
Guardian Angel 32
Dying Soul 33
Shared Pain 34
Sweet Solitude 35
Undefeated 36
Mr. Nice 37
Farewell to Misery 38
Foolish Heart 39

A Promise 40
Uncertainty 41
Nightly Sky 42
Defeated Limitations 43
A Silent Oath 44
Pure Clarity 45
Champion 46
Perseverance 47
A battle to remember 49
Ignorance 50
Kindred Spirit 51
Inner Child 52
Internal Strength 53

Chapter 3: A Look to Yesteryears 55

The Messenger 56
Beware 57
Telemechus's Letter 58
Penelope's Prayer 59
Three Hundred 60
Mother Greece 61
Cinderella 62

Birth of a Dream

Ah, to those that are near
Witness the birth of a dream.
Listen to the story I tell,
One that brings tears
To the eyes of the fierce.

Listen to the words
That yesterday were dreams.
Ah, misery had left him stranded.

Failed attempts seemed normal.
Never did surrender cross his mind
Like a general he stuck to his mission.
Some called him a dreamer
Others laughed obnoxiously.

Call it a miracle or a sign
These gloomy skies found sunlight
His dream revealed for all to see
Ah, a sunset can't compare
To the smile upon his face.
Finally the flower has blossomed,
In front of his very eyes
Breathes his creation.

CHAPTER 1: THROUGH THESE LENSES

Through These Lenses

Through these lenses
Dark skies are seen.
Filled with ambiguity
Dreams lost in the wind.
Joy silently waves
As it waits patiently.
Tears in a mother's eyes
Fall like rain drops
Dreaded loneliness
Found another victim.
Suffering stands unchallenged
In a world with broken promises.
Despair and all his guests
Reserve a table of five.
In a heart that aches
From the ruthless reality.
Eyes that see such madness
Spare me for just a moment.

To the Poet

A flower amongst thorns
mastering his craft.
To you who speak
Words of the very heart,
You, who allows his pen
To write what couldn't be told.

Oh you are unique and rare
Never do you ask for support.
You follow the less traveled road
An overdue thank you I must say
For you are one of those dreamers
That make life so magnificent.
You bring emotions to life
Through many forms.
Oh, a poet is a warrior
Protecting the world nightly.
To you the poet I speak
When I say a job well done.

Standing Ovation

Your finest
Production
Questions you.

Scribbling on a pad
As anger flows
In my veins.

You sell normality
Well, I am fine
With insanity.

Play in
My sandpit
Then tell me
I'm not sane.

Be mislabeled
Disrespected
Used
And judged.

Lose
Every
Yard gained.

Hide your
Sweaty palms
In pockets
Of embarrassment.

Shall I
Applaud
Or stand
In shame?

Dear Mr. President

Some have failed miserably.
Others have left legacies.
Newly elected president,
A moment is all I require.
Presented to you is a daunting task
Upon your shoulders lays a weight
One that is not to be taken lightly.

We look to you for guidance
As we witness history.
I write this not to stir debate
Rather to ease the minds of many
I beg of thee to remember promises.

To those who face misfortune,
Remind them of the American dream.
A fine example lies in you
The son of immigrants,
Now leading the free world.

Aside from state events
There are challenges that wait.
Keep calm and poignant.
Show no act of surrender.
Never forget those who elected you.
Mr. President, will you leave a legacy?

Political Prostitution

Perfection
Is sold
On
Campaign
Trails.

In
Honest
Voices
They
Promise
Everything
Short
Of
Paradise.

Influenced
By
Special Interests.

Sexual Scandals
Bribery
Embezzlement
Unworthy wars.

Maybe that
Should be
A slogan
That
Sticks.

Health care
Reform
Better economy
Bringing our
Troops

Back.

On the
Last
Page
Of
An unread
Agenda.

A Simple Song

Excuse me,
Will you play a song?
Our troubles may you ease
Through the strings of your guitar
For a moment take us away
To a land unknown.

Oh, play that song tonight,
Make our hearts find hope.
Erase our anguish with
Your marvelous voice.

Dazzle us with your words
Spread our wings with
Hope of a better world
Mister, thank you for finding joy
Where darkness lives.
Kind sir, will you play next week
For those who need a simple song?

Weary Traveler

Filled with tainted hope,
He enters the cab.

"Where to?" asks the driver.
Ironically, he has no preference.
All he wants is to be heard.
The cab driver sees him torn.
"So, what's on your mind?"

The weary traveler starts to sob,
He swallows his pride.
The cab driver drives into the night.
New York City traffic and skyscrapers
Can be seen from his window.

Suddenly he speaks of a woman
That left him to count the hours.
He doesn't wait for sympathy,
He continues as the tears fall.
The driver feels his pain
As he tells him to be strong,
Even if weakness seems tempting.
He tells him to forget yesterday.
Tomorrow waits with much more.

A Day in New York

The radiant sun watches
A city lost in an addicting routine
Overcome by New York City's rush hour,
Leaving no time for self discovery.

Energized by overpriced coffee,
Sounds of disgruntled cab drivers
Can be heard throughout the city,
Lost in the beauty of Broadway plays.

Amazed by the adrenaline rush
That rattles one's inner being,
Surrounded by skyscrapers
Filled with breathtaking views,
Tempted by oven fresh pizza
Found in the streets of little Italy,
Protected by Lady Liberty herself,
Such beauty can only be found
In the streets of New York.

No Surprise

Extra, extra
Read all about it:
Members of Congress,
Entrusted statesmen
Who now became investors
In failing corporations.

What about the man
That lost his fortunes
Waiting on unemployment?
Is he not a citizen
Of this great nation?

Did you forget your duties
Of representing your delegates
And not your best interests?

Put your hands together, America,
For the ones you elected
Left you stranded.

American Dream

Excitement rushes
At speeds unimaginable
Through this young man.

In search of prosperity,
Embarking on a journey
That is life altering.

Five dollars in his pockets,
Ready to embrace opportunities
That yesterday seemed impossible.

His heart spoke loudly.
America was no longer a dream.
It was waiting with open arms.

As he landed in his new home,
He hid a tear from the world.
Some angel answered his prayer.
No more broken dreams,
Time to leave a legacy.
A simple education
And determination to prosper.
His story is one to remember
When in doubt of dreams.

A Moment

Paradise seems
So close
In your
Hazel eyes.

Your warm arms
Are my safety
In a ruthless
Realm of existence.

You must be
A product
Of God's finest work.
I pray unto him
To keep you
Safe from harm.

No currency
Is valid
When it comes
To buying your
Flawless beauty.

No army is a match.
As for generals,
They fall victim
Slowly, to your lips
Filled with hope.

Princess, Goddess
Of my world.
May you spare
A moment
With little ole me.

Actress

Dressed in devilish red
With lips that baptize
All who dare to kiss them.

Eyes promising desire,
Innocence replaced by lust,
Magical smile that entices,

Actress in a play of deceit.
Those who watch - left speechless.
As she bows, the audience trembles.

She smirks at some helpless man
That drowns in her oceans,
Mesmerized by her elegance.
Ah, the actress that toils
Will one day play her part.

Adrenaline

Palms drenched in sweat,
Anxiety, a raging creature
Left in your stomach.
Nausea telling you to quit,
Adrenaline offering excitement,
Confusion crowds your mind.

Time to leave them breathless,
Critics watching for mistakes,
Pressure drastically escalates,
Dreams reached the stage.

You're almost there -
Will you take on the fight?
Or will you pack your things?
Hurry up, you only have seconds!
Will you let them win?

At Peace

He sat in his favorite rocking chair,
Looking aimlessly at the empty room.
Simplicity never felt so right.
You could see him smile from afar
As yesterday came to mind.

The doctor gave him the facts,
Sixty-five years threatened by cancer.
He gathered his grandchildren near
As he told them how much he loved them.
Dinner and the usual chatter,
He shed a tear from his eyes.
In his heart he knew that his
Time card needed to be checked in
"Gramps," said his granddaughter,
"No need to cry."

If they only knew his woes
And how they wouldn't go away.
He tucked in the young ones.
As he looked at old photos
Of his dear departed wife,
He told her that he was on his way.

Monster

Covered with
Smothering insecurities,
He watches as his life
Pours into another glass.
He tries to fight the urge
As he allows weakness
Entrance into his world.

Drop by drop,
Looking for excuses.
He finds the same one.
"Just another sip,"
He says without hesitation.
Temptation celebrates.

Winning an unchallenged fight,
Joy is felt for a second.
Then pain opens its doors.
Friends are a hassle,
Work is meaningless.

His breath smells
Of last night's whiskey.
Rent is past due.
Drastically life worsens
As the urge grows.
Now he wishes
He could muster
Strength to beat
His growing monster.

Russian Roulette

Standing on the ledge and asking
If life will be better without him;
Covered in self-destruction,
As he plays Russian roulette.
Tonight he needs no opponent.

He screams, but the bystanders
Seem to be over occupied.
From the anxiety he shivers.
No need to hide emotions
When no one cares to notice.

The cell phone in his pocket
Won't stop ringing.
Oh, they want to listen!
Well, it doesn't work like that.
His mind speaks, but his heart
Waves a white flag.

"Should I jump?" he asks loudly.
A crying mother screams NO.
The proud father, on his knees,
Asks God to save his boy.
Emotions race as reality stares
Into dark eyes that lost hope.
He wanted to be heard
What a price to pay.

Your Performance

To the sound of applause
You enter the well-lit stage.
As you take a deep breath,
The crowd screams your name,
As your words pour themselves
Into so many hearts.
Tears fall from your eyes,
For the excitement is painted
On the faces of the masses.
As your performance concludes,
Many ask you to carry on.
Time becomes less significant;
Your words become vaccines
To the demons of a raging pain.
Like the sound of Apollo's Lyre,
You leave your listeners in awe.
Their hearts become a canvas
Which you fill with masterpieces.

Predators

Blind to the escalating
Predators that live among us,
Spreading incurable viruses
That penetrate brain waves
Of innocent citizens.

To an overzealous corporation
All we are is guinea pigs
Stripped of our thinking process.
Left to invade emergency rooms,
Medicating our seeds with Tami flu
Rather than facing a dark reality.
One that would leave victims
With the ability to see past
The prairies of corruption
And into the desperate need
Of an election that would filter
The dirt and leave us pure once more.

Collateral Damage

Bullets spraying overhead,
Watching comrades beg
For their very lives,
Praying to see another sunrise.

Trying to keep on task,
All you have is a picture
That you hold tightly.
Nightmares keep you awake,
Remembering the promises made
To your wife and children.

The ebony sky
Slowly lights up
From bombs dropping.
Your life flashes in front
Of your eyes.

Another brother
Put in a coffin.
Hours seem endless
Keep telling yourself
That you will go home alive.

Classified section

Left to fend on his own
Without a simple
Thank you

Dreams become dust
As he is let go
Twenty five years
Ended in a moment

A man's worst nightmare
Is when he can't
Provide for his family
His son looks at him
As he reads classified ads
In the newspaper

His wife comes home sobbing
Both credit cards declined
As they resort to the jar
Titled petty cash

He tries to keep composure
As he works odd jobs
To pay the bills

Who knew he would
End up like this
In America?

Forgotten Boulevards

Walking on boulevards
That are forgotten,
Filled with hope
And all that comes with it.

In this city of broken promises
Aimlessly I continue to wander,
Searching for castles in the sand.

Lost in the oceans of despair
As I search for land.
Stranded in the alleys
That keep me far from
All I once knew.

At the bottom of the bottle
I scream but no one answers.
When will I find the one
I left behind…

Unspoken

In his favorite recliner
He holds his grandson.
As the sun slowly sets
His grandson curiously asks
"Grandpa, did you ever go to war?"

He smiles and says "Yes."
The child asks how it was.
With a tear in his eyes he looks away
And says it was brutally unbearable.
The child can't imagine
As the grandfather tells him
That America called upon him
To fight for freedom.
Bombs, gunshots and carnage,
Watching grown men cry.
His grandson is shocked.
"It was a mess," he says.
The grandfather says, "Now run along."

As the child does so, the phone rings.
It is his army buddy.
They speak for hours.
One thing they don't mention
Is those they left behind.

THROUGH THESE LENSES

CHAPTER 2: WINDOWS OF A SOUL

The Few Good Hearted

When darkness presides
Their compassion shines brightly.
Oh, they are larger than life
For they tend to a broken heart.
In one's moment of distress
They offer to genuinely care
And in this day and age
Such action is deemed unlikely.
Call them guardian angels
Or good Samaritans
That make pain obsolete.
Oh, they are truly a blessing
To a world lost in misfortunes.
These words are written
In honor of the few goodhearted.

Lady Love

Against the mistress love
No army stands a chance.
The strongest of hearts decay,
Courage left weaponless.

From her there is no safe haven
Nightly she invades weak minds.
Her laughter is almost taunting
Slowly she poisons her victims.

Beware of her hypnotizing smile
Pay no mind to her luscious lips
Forget her angelic innocence.

She promises all that is heavenly
Then she lets you slowly burn.
No currency can persuade her,
A criminal left uncaptured.

Guardian Angel

Like autumn leaves
You scattered away
To unknown galaxies.
Your presence crowds
The corners of my mind.
Your angelic smile is found
In this world's darkest alleys.
The armies of deception
Surrender to your voice,
The one that crowds churches.
A summer sun on green pastures
Can be found in your blue eyes.
Your fragile fingertips cure
The deadliest of diseases.
A kiss from your very lips
Cleanses all who sin.
Your laughter soothes
The worst of heartaches.
You are my guardian angel.

Dying Soul

Somewhere deep
In the pits of a dying soul
Lives a will to be nourished.
A simple hello seems miraculous,
Pity's canvas is not blank this night.

Mountains of dreams tumble down
Into deserts of self-doubt.
Heroes seem like clay figures
That await a breath of life.

Influenced by tendencies
Governing a weak mind.
Insecurities become savages
Roaming freely in the valleys
Of an inescapable past.

A beating heart
Through ink speaks
Pure emotions that
Bring one to his knees.

Shared Pain

Tell me of your troubles.
Friend, why the long face?
I promise not to speak a word,
No need to hide your tears
When you're amongst friends.

Spill every ounce of pain
And I will carry your burdens
Through the ages of life,
Know that you are loved
And that your pain is shared.

Let my words be your remedy
If the climb is too steep
Count on me to be there
When the world seems dark.
Let my smile offer guidance.
No thank you is required,
Only a simple promise
That you will never
Leave me stranded.

Sweet Solitude

In these hours
Of utter confusion
I seek a helping hand.
Weakness resides in this heart.

In words I find refuge,
Through them I slowly heal.

A man who is challenged
Is asked to be his true self.
Truth is a package easily lost.
Blinded pride is comforting
Until it finds vision.

Regrets quickly race
In ways unimagined.
Sweet solitude is but a dream
In this world of total chaos.
Lady Justice sheds a tear
As she watches over us.
When that inner voice speaks
There's no point in ignoring it.

Undefeated

Attached to the strings
Of a single puppeteer,
In search of hope
That slithered away.

Filled with uncertainty
That grows stronger.
Lost in the mediocrity
That seems normal.
Mountains of sorrow
Discreetly multiplied;
Joy feels untouched
Like a dusty picture frame.
Dreams slowly lose to the
Single judgment of another.
Love has lost the rose petals
To a mistress named lust.

Speechlessly passion
Wanders into the night -
Thankfully a strand of faith
Resides in the basement
Of a lost soul's heart.

Mr. Nice

Sorry, but I had a change of heart,
Mr. Nice Guy chose to depart,
How do you like me this day?
Now that I put my smile away.

You must be proud of me,
The man you thought I should be.
Pen, show no mercy this night,
This time I will take on the fight.
Keep feeding me your denial,
I won't need a lawyer in this trial,
For I am already paying the price,
My crime was being Mr. Nice.

Come, and don't shed a tear,
This man you will now learn to fear.
Filled with anger and so much rage
Emotions pour slowly on this page.
Put your hands together for what you built,
A little too late for tears of guilt.

Farewell to Misery

I welcome you no more,
I will not be a victim.
Listen to my words
As they bid you farewell.
No more shall my eyes
Resort to unwanted tears.
Spare me the torment,
This moment I seek solidarity,
Not pity from a single man.
Don't forget to take the pain
That leaves me weary.
Oh, would you leave my skies
Cloudless and bright?
Is this too much to ask
From a man on his knees?
Let me learn of joy;
May it be welcome.

Foolish Heart

Eyes that promised paradise
Left you in the pits of hell
Oh, foolish heart,
Won't you learn
The ways of betrayal?
Why did I listen?
Now I live in agony.

Endless hours allow memories
To invade my weak mind.
Heart, will you hide your tears?
We will find a smile,
Even if it is impossible,
An angel will captivate you.
You'll beg of me to take notice.
Promise me one thing,
That she won't be like her.

A Promise

Another bridge to cross
In the midst of a storm.
Stick to the plan -
Even if it debilitates
Your soul.

Show no sign
Of despair.
Put aside
That white flag,
For surrender
Is a path
That will not be
Taken on this day.

A man is measured
Through his actions -
Failure is a stone
Best left unturned.

No need for tears -
Let my shoulders carry you.
Just promise me one thing,
That you will carry on.

Uncertainty

Strength through words -
May I offer?
Dark days are upon us,
Uncertainty leaves you defenseless
In the absence of others.

Contemplating what tomorrow provides -
All you want is sincerity
From those trusted.
Ironically, they left you stranded.

Faith is what keeps your smile -
In your eyes, despair found residence.
What if you stood as a man?
No more waiting on miracles,
Time to forget misery.

Be sturdy and hide no truth -
You are as worthy as the next man.
Don't lose the will to attain,
Keep on the road you chose.
The sun will guide you once more.
Until then, never lose sight
Of all that brings a smile.

Nightly Sky

Nightly sky that is home
To my guiding stars.
Send me on unending voyages
That leave me at her door step.
Safely let her sleep to the sound
Of the waves hitting the sand.

If she dreams of me,
Send her hope.
If she sheds a single tear,
Sing her a lullaby
That calms all who listen.

Oh, guiding star, I beg you
To take me to her bedside
Where pain is not welcome.
Let me drown in her eyes.
Oh, nightly sky, defeat the sunrise.
Every dream brings me nearer
To my angel with broken wings.

Defeated Limitations

Emotions ooze
From my very pores
Into the empty chapters
Of my destiny.

As I look life in the eyes
I start to shiver slowly.
Adversity, a gift and a curse.
Tears are said to show weakness,
Well, then let shame shower me.

Lost in the mazes of uncertainty,
Hope is my only course of action.
Awaiting another horizon to dawn,
Indulging in endless thoughts.

Filled with passion and optimism,
Energized by defeated limitations,
Molded by the sound of denial,
Grateful for the opportunity to write
From a heart that sings psalms of hope.

A Silent Oath

Mirror on the wall,
Solemnly swear to me
Not to speak of my anguish
Nor take notice of my dismay.

Keep silent to the curious lady -
Slowly even she departed.
Of her I speak no malice -
I ask you to keep her strong
As I embark on this hollow ship.

Keep my distress hidden in gardens,
For pity is no recipe for a true man.
Let my maker keep me close
If I don't return home,
Shed no tears, my close friend.

I promise to never forget thee,
Like the ones that left me wounded,
I speak no more as I bid you farewell.
Remember the oath you took this day.

Pure Clarity

In these hours of turmoil
Much burdens my heart.
Dismay clouds my mind,
Uncertainty shines brightly,
Hope has no say this night.

Therefore I seek
A moment of pure clarity
To put aside malicious thoughts,
Allow faith to dry tears,
For once more we will prevail.

Our voices shall be heard.
Another gloomy sky
Shall not be seen.
We will not allow rage
As a guest in our homes,
Nor will we allow pain
To infect our veins.

Champion

Dressed in shades of grey
As I encounter rejection.
No, I will not ignore aspirations
For another's pleasure.
The Lord gave me mountains;
I shall climb them proudly,
Even if some steer me away,
I will not lose my faith.
For the victory I yearn
Will be in my grasp soon.

They say failure is destiny.
As my blood boils,
I seek to challenge them.
Yes, the one they classify unworthy
Asks them to step in his shoes,
Live with his flaws.
Do they think they can prevail?

I am not different but unique.
See, my flaws are my strengths,
Every breath is a testimony
To those who thought otherwise.
As if they knew my challenges.

No person shall get in my way,
For a dream is something I won't lose.
Call me anything you choose,
Epileptic or learning disabled.
But remember that
I am the one
Who reached his goal.

Perseverance

The window
Of a soul
Shows clouds
Filled with tears.

Strength is
A yesterday
That stands alone
In a crowded room.

A flawless passion
Burns slowly
In the hearts of few.

Lost in commotion
Is one known as hope.
Quietly he cries
For he is left
Helpless.
In the dungeons
Of agony
Lives a peasant
Known as joy.
His destiny
Turns bleak
At one's will.

Perseverance
Stands emotionless
In a duel with
The force of darkness.

Slowly the clouds
Dismantle
As adrenaline
Resurrects

Innocence
From Hades.

A battle to remember

A victory is yearned
From an inner enemy.
A new sun rises,
Old memories crowd
A wandering mind.
Tears fall like rain drops.

He has many names,
Call him depression
Or even Mr. Anxiety.
How he creeps up
In the quiet of night.
No law can protect you
From his unending reign.
Sweat moistens your palms
As they shake uncontrollably.
Your heart races as you try
To defeat a strong foe.

Hope becomes a broken glass.
There has to be a better way.
Oh, this will not be accepted.
Smiles will be worn,
Even if the pain is unbearable.
Slave to this unleashed demon,
For how long can one be?
One must be stronger than the
Devil who taunts relentlessly.
If he wants an unchallenged fight,
It will be a battle to remember.

Ignorance

In time of need
We turn to a higher being
To answer our call.
When the world turns away,
For some reason we curse faith.

Were we not given free will
To attain all desired?
Are we not forgiven for our actions?
Is man not in search of perfection?
When will we realize life
Is a blank page waiting to be written?

A fist is so easy to clench
Compared to the act of understanding,
Made by the same creator.
Somehow we continue to ignore
The man with nothing to give
That is blinded by agony.

When will we comprehend
The simplicity of forgiveness?
Ironically a weapon solves disputes.

Kindred Spirit

The wind
Scattered the pieces
Of his kindred spirit.

Alone he gathers
Thoughts of yesterday
That keep him awake
When the world sleeps.

A suitcase with nothing
But broken dreams
Kept by his bedside.

Never does he question
The cards he was dealt.
The bitter world
Left him gasping for air.

Defenseless and weary,
He fell victim to
Demons that know
No mercy.

He would give the world
To let the winter snow melt
From his
Troubled face.

Inner Child

Why the tears?
Show that smile,
The one that cures pain.
Let your heart
Be soothed by these words
Of a hope left untouched.

Know that no worry
Is worth the loss of a grin.
Friend, let the better you
A moment to shine.

No need to live in yesterday
When today is waiting.
Put aside those dark thoughts
As a new day is embraced.

Be the one who you want to be,
Set your wings and fly into the
Fairy tales that make life grand.
Listen to your inner child's voice
As it jumps and yells of joy.

Internal Strength

Eyes fill with many tears,
Victimized by my fears.
To whom should I speak?
I can't show how I am weak.

Lost in the coldest of nights
With my reflection I start fights,
Asking why I can't be stronger,
Doubting if I can hold on any longer.

Allowing strangers to walk all over me,
This is not who I was supposed to be,
Condemned to a galaxy of self denial,
My passion waits to walk the aisle.

As for my heart, it is used to being torn.
To the Lord, I ask for a hero to be born.
Surrounding are thoughts of doubt.
My internal demons continue to shout.

Weakness showers me with negativity,
My soul whispers of creativity.
It reminds me of a yesterday.
Even my pen wants a better way.

The hero I was waiting for has arrived.
In the darkest of days, this man has survived.
He tells me to stand and never let go.
He helped by never saying no.

I cried; this man was my inner strength.

CHAPTER 3: A LOOK TO YESTERYEARS

The Messenger

As I ramble on
Of my yesteryears
Pay no mind
To me, oh sir.
I seek not much,
Only a simple favor if you will.
Will you find the one I yearn for?
Tell her of my battered self.
No, don't leave her uninformed,
Fall on your bare knees and promise
All that is heavenly and sacred.
Hasten like Hermes himself,
Take no moment of rest.
Every night she keeps me awake…
Be on your way, my entrusted messenger.
Hold her words far from preying eyes.
May the heavens protect you -
Now embark upon your voyage.

Beware

I am but a slave
Therefore, I am unworthy.
Oh, mighty Caesar,
I come to you this day
Bearing news of caution.
Still I will speak this
That troubles me.

You will be betrayed.
Oh, Hades shall you meet
In the halls of the Senate.
Your blood will flow freely.
Oh, worthy Caesar, the murderer
Is one you hold in deep regard,
One that goes by the name Brutus.

May the gods offer you wisdom.
The day nears, act in haste
Or Rome will lose a son.

Telemechus's Letter

Oh, wise father Odysseus;
Listen to words of your son.
I ask of thee to offer council
As I pray for your safe return.

Uninvited suitors torment mother.
They eat of our food,
Drink of our wine.
No woman deserves this,
Let alone a royal queen.

In Poseidon's oceans do you linger
Or has mighty Zeus cursed you?
Have you fallen amongst comrades?

I will search lands and oceans alike
Until I find you, oh glorious father,
Your stories shall be read in all lands.
Let the gods grant you strength.

Shall I mourn you, oh mighty king,
Or will Athena bring you to Ithaca's shores?
If so, we shall celebrate and feast,
Make offering to the gods,
Punish those who leave mother in tears.
May they see a painful death.

Oh father, long has Ithaca waited
For their Odysseus to come home.

Penelope's Prayer

All knowing Zeus,
I beg of you
To tell me of Odysseus.

Did he fall
In the city of Troy?
Was he properly mourned
Or left stranded?

Suitors await my answer.
Within I feel he shall return
To the rugged land of Ithaca.
My poor son asks for him.
God of gods, show me a sign,
Bring our king to his palace.

I offer you libations and prayer.
Show my Odysseus the route
That will erase all his woes.

Ah, show no ounce of mercy
To those suitors that
Wait to have me as their wife!
Grant me this, all powerful Zeus.

Three Hundred

Gather near
Fellow Spartans.
Today our swords
Are called upon.
Let every Greek
Know of Thermopolis
As the greatest battle.
Let Persian blood
Stain this field.
Persian tyranny
Will not torment any Greek.
Together we shall fight
Until the last Persian dies.
May the gods be with us.

Mother Greece

From the steps of the Parthenon
I bow to you oh mother Greece.
Bathed in your clear oceans,
Refreshed from your sweet wine,
Surrounded by unimaginable beauty,
Protected by the swords of Sparta,
Intrigued by wise Plato and Socrates,
Entertained by Sophocles himself.

At your town squares you can hear
Of politics, gossip and all you desire
In its music lives passion.

Oh mother Greece, dressed like Athena
What a sight are your lovely ports.
Sunsets as the ones of Santorin
Have lovers lost in fairy tales.
Oh hail Queen of the Aegean
Seductress of passion and beauty,
May solace be found in your future.

Cinderella

The clock strikes twelve
As her lips intoxicate me
With flattery.
She takes me to paradise.

To the sound of her voice
Heavenly angels dance.
In her hazel eyes
Fantasies become realities.
With her gentle touch
She leaves me breathless.

If only I knew who she was,
I would call her near.
As I fell on my bare knees,
I would savor the moment
And in my heart it wouldn't end.

For such a jewel is priceless.
She left so quickly,
Dressed like a princess.
A smile that brightens
The underworld.
She will be missed.

www.ingramcontent.com/pod-product-compliance
Lightning Source LLC
Chambersburg PA
CBHW051715040426
42446CB00008B/891